BRITISH RAILWAYS

PAST and PRESENT

No 50

Map of the railways of North Staffordshire, showing locations featured or referred to in the text.

BRITISH RAILWAYS

PAST and PRESENT

No 50

North Staffordshire

Hugh Ballantyne

Past and
Present

Past & Present Publishing Ltd

First published in 2005

British Library Cataloguing in Publication Data

A catalogue record for this book is available from the British Library.

ISBN 1 85895 204 2

Past & Present Publishing Ltd
The Trundle
Ringstead Road
Great Addington
Kettering
Northants NN14 4BW

Tel/Fax: 01536 330588
email: sales@nostalgiacollection.com
Website: www.nostalgiacollection.com

Printed and bound in Great Britain

ACKNOWLEDGEMENTS

Not only am I extremely grateful to all the photographers who have loaned me material for this book, without which it could not have been produced, but also to the many other people who have generously given me the benefit of their time, assistance and advice. These include Allan C. Baker, John Bucknall, Roy Burnett, Richard Casserley, Geoffrey Dingle, Colin Gall, David Holroyde, Robert Moorcroft, Nelson Twells, Martin Welch, John Williams and Greg Wilson. Finally, I would like to thank various members of the Churnet Valley Railway and the Rudyard Lake Steam Railway for their courtesy and unfailing assistance.

STONE: Coming south over the junction points at Stone, 'Converted Royal Scot' No 46162 *Queen's Westminster Rifleman* makes a fine sight working the 10.05am Manchester to Euston express on 4 September 1954.

The Colwich line platforms and signal box have been removed and the goods shed, no longer in railway use, looks much the worse for wear as Virgin Trains 'Pendolino' No 390037 passes with the 12.15 Manchester to Euston service on 12 April 2005. *H. C. Casserley/HB*

CONTENTS

Introduction   7

West Coast Main Line:
   Madeley to Rugeley Trent Valley   9
Potteries main line:
   Harecastle to Norton Bridge and Colwich   38
Potteries loop line   61
Newcastle Junction to Silverdale   72
Biddulph Valley line to Stoke Junction
   and Leek Brook Junction   77
Leek Brook Junction to Waterhouses and the
   Leek & Manifold Valley Light Railway   84
Churnet Valley line   94
Stoke to Uttoxeter and the Cheadle Railway   109
Stafford to Uttoxeter   121

Index of locations   128

INTRODUCTION

This book, the 50th in the 'British Railways Past and Present' series, only covers a small geographical region, the northern part of Staffordshire, but it is an area of great contrast and diversity in town and country and in the three pre-Grouping railways that served it. Industry came relatively early to the region as pottery-making became established in the 18th century in villages to the east of the market town of Newcastle-under-Lyme, with coal-mining and iron-smelting developing to the north-west of the town and limestone-quarrying in the moorlands of the high ground to the east. These industries required transport, causing canals and tramroads to be promoted, the Trent & Mersey Canal of 1777 being of prime importance. Into the 19th century, with early railway schemes formulated, it was not until 1837 that the first long-distance railway came into being when the Grand Junction Railway from Newton Junction to Birmingham passed north to south through the county, serving Stafford, the county town. This was the first long-distance – or inter-city – railway in England, and within nine years had joined with two neighbouring railways, the London & Birmingham and the Manchester & Birmingham, to form what became the largest pre-Grouping railway in Great Britain, the London & North Western Railway.

The industrial 'Potteries' were still without rail connection until local industrialists, chaired by Robert Heathcote, sought to promote railways into the area, but it was not until 1848, following opposition by conflicting canal interests, that the North Staffordshire Railway connected Stoke-on-Trent with other lines at Norton Bridge and Burton-on-Trent. This railway gave further impetus to the manufacturing Potteries in the 'Six Towns', namely Tunstall, Burslem, Hanley, Stoke, Fenton and Longton (not 'Five Towns', as made famous in the tales of the area by novelist Arnold Bennett). In addition to the traditional heavy industries of coal-mining, iron-and-steel-making and pottery, there were also two locomotive manufacturers: the North Staffordshire Railway built some of its own locomotives at Stoke, and close by was the works of Kerr, Stuart & Co, where locomotives were built for both home and overseas markets.

Surrounding the Potteries there is contrasting rural scenery in North Staffordshire that often surprises first-time visitors with its natural beauty. The West Coast Main Line sweeps into the county off the Cheshire Plain near the Maer Hills and down through a pleasing mixed agricultural region of neat farms and hedgerows following the streams that flow into the River Trent south of Stafford. To the north-east of the Potteries there is attractive countryside around Lake Rudyard, which had been heavily promoted by the NSR 'for rest and recreation', while to the south of the lake there is the Churnet Valley, a popular area that, in addition to its natural beauty, has the added interest of the preserved steam Churnet Valley Railway and the Caldon Canal. East from there is the high moorland country, hidden away in which is the outstandingly beautiful Manifold Valley, ideal for walking now that the lamented Leek &

STOKE-ON-TRENT was the headquarters of the former North Staffordshire Railway and in BR days a Divisional Manager's region. This is a view looking north from the main up platform in 1956, showing a thriving railway in its industrial setting. From the left there are the down sidings, Stoke North signal box and to the right of the main lines the carriage sidings and a Stanier 2-6-4T shunting. To the right of this engine is the façade of North Staffordshire college and in the background some distinctive bottle-shaped buildings, known locally as 'pot-banks'; these are kilns used in the pottery industry for which the area was, and still is, justifiable famous.

On 3 April 2005 we see today's basic railway. Everything to the left has been swept away and on the right all the sidings have gone, leaving just a short stub. The platform has been extended slightly, but to the right the railway land has been converted into a car park. The only new feature in the middle is Stoke power box alongside which Virgin Trains 'Voyager' No 221141 is approaching as the 10.24 Manchester to Birmingham service. On the extreme right the college building has now become part of Staffordshire University. *Martin Welch/HB*

Manifold Light Railway has long been closed. The south of the area covered by this book had a small part of the third of the three pre-Grouping railways referred to in the text, namely the Great Northern Railway, which served a rural district of small villages east of Stafford towards Uttoxeter. The railway junction town of Stafford itself was prosperous, with salt-mining and heavy industry, among which English Electric made heavy electrical equipment and W. G. Bagnall Ltd built locomotives.

In 1910 the 'Six Towns' merged to become the County Borough of Stoke-on-Trent, and in 1926, on a visit to the Potteries, King George V conferred City status upon it.

Finally, for continuity in the text of this book please note that where appropriate, for the power and name classification of LMS-owned locomotives, I have used the 1946 modernisation programme designations, and for brevity I trust readers from Stoke-on-Trent will not mind their city being simply referred to as Stoke.

Hugh Ballantyne, Eccleshall, Stafford

BIBLIOGRAPHY

Baker, Allan C. *The Cheadle Railway* (Oakwood Press, 1979)
   The Potteries Loop Line (Trent Valley Publications, 1986)
Christiansen, Rex *A Regional History of the Railways of Great Britain*, Vol 7 West Midlands
   (David & Charles, 1973)
Christiansen, Rex and Miller R. W. *The North Staffordshire Railway* (David & Charles, 1971)
Cobb, Col M. H. *The Railways of Great Britain – A Historical Atlas* (Ian Allan Publishing, 2003)
Gammell, C. J. *LMS Branch Lines* (GRQ Publications, 1988)
   LNER Branch Lines (Oxford Publishing Co, 1994)
Jenkins, S. C. *The Leek & Manifold Valley Light Railway* (Oakwood Press, 1991)
Jeuda, Basil *Memories of the North Staffordshire Railway* (Cheshire Libraries 1986)
   The Knotty (Lightmoor Press, 1996)
   The Leek, Caldon & Waterhouses Railway (North Staffordshire Railway Co, 1980)
Keys, R. and NSR Society *The Churnet Valley Railway* (Moorland Publishing, 1974)
Keys, R. and Porter, L. *The Manifold Valley and its Light Railway* (Moorland Publishing, 1972)
Lester, C. R. *The Stoke to Market Drayton Line* (Oakwood Press, 1983)
Talbot, E. *Railways in and around Stafford* (Foxline Publishing, 1994)
Webster, Norman *Britain's First Trunk Line* (Adams & Dart, 1972)

Back issues of
British Railways Illustrated
Railway Bylines
The Railway Magazine
Railway Observer
The Sentinel (Stoke-on-Trent)
Steam Days

West Coast Main Line:
Madeley to Rugeley Trent Valley

MADELEY: The West Coast Main Line (WCML) sweeps south into Staffordshire, coming off the Cheshire Plain into a wide open fertile valley after a steady climb from Crewe. This is a fine vintage picture of Madeley station, taken circa 1900, looking south, showing its spacious layout with four platforms serving the fast and slow lines. This section of the WCML is part of one of England's earliest and most historic railways, the Grand Junction Railway from Newton Junction to Birmingham, opened on 4 July 1837, which amalgamated with the London & Birmingham and Manchester & Birmingham to become the London & North Western Railway (LNWR) in July 1846.

The station was closed to passengers on 4 February 1952 and all trace of it has gone except for a small length of brick wall on the right, which was at the back of the down slow platform. The overhead structures of the 25Kv electrification dominate the scene on 6 April 2005, but the track alignment remains remarkably similar. Electric train services from Manchester and Liverpool on this part of the WCML as far south as Stafford commenced on 7 January 1963. *John K Williams collection/HB*

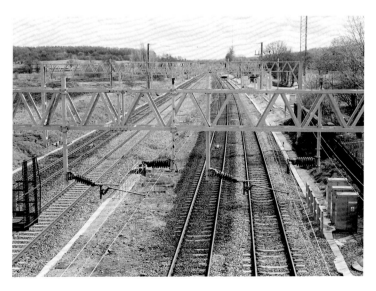

WHITMORE WATER TROUGHS, situated just north of Whitmore station, were laid in the 1860s. This is a view looking north towards Crewe showing 'Converted Royal Scot' No 46130 *The West Yorkshire Regiment* on the up fast line in about 1962 with water cascading over the back of the tender. The 25Kv electrification wires and supports are already complete and will soon render the water troughs and splendid scenes such as this redundant.

There is now no trace of the water troughs and even locomotive-hauled passenger trains are becoming increasingly rare on the route. Today Virgin Trains operate all the WCML services to and from Euston using electric 'Pendolino' units, such as No 390035, seen here forming the 12.15 Liverpool to Euston service on 6 April 2005. *John B. Bucknall/HB*

WHITMORE WATER TROUGHS: Looking south from the same location towards the site of the former Whitmore station, a Stanier Class 5 is starting to pick up water from the down fast line working a Birmingham to Manchester train in about 1962. When opened in 1837, together with Wolverhampton, Stafford, Crewe, Hartford and Warrington, Whitmore station, situated in the small village of Baldwins Gate, was classified as a First Class Station. The reason for its importance lay in the fact that it was then the nearest point at which horse-drawn buses could connect the Potteries towns and Shrewsbury with the railway. Once these places became railway connected, Whitmore's importance quickly declined.

At the same location Central Trains EMU No 170398 passes by with the 12.21 Birmingham to Liverpool service on 6 April 2005. *John B Bucknall/HB*

STANDON BRIDGE: At Whitmore the railway curves to avoid the Maer Hills and comes down into the valley of the Meece Brook towards Standon Bridge station. Just north of there 'Converted Royal Scot' No 46110 *Grenadier Guardsman* passes the hamlet of Cranberry on the up fast line with the 10.05am Glasgow to Birmingham express on 18 February 1961.

Electrification gantries block the present-day scene but the houses behind the smoke of the engine in the 'past' picture remain the same. Otherwise the main changes are the removal of the wartime Nissen huts and the erection of the ugly and excessive steel palisade bounding the railway, as a Virgin Trains 'Voyager' unit comes south on the up fast line on 6 April 2005. *Both HB*

STANDON BRIDGE station (closed on 4 February 1952) was situated this side of the overbridge seen behind the train, a northbound mixed goods hauled by clean Stanier Class 5 No 45374 on 18 February 1961. Note the well-maintained non-welded track and the neatly trimmed lineside, particularly on the right.

Surprisingly in this day and age the trackside at this location remains remarkably clean, tidy and clear of vegetation. Virgin Trains 'Pendolino' No 390041 speeds north working the 12.45 Euston to Preston service on 6 April 2005. *Both HB*

BADNALL WHARF: At milepost 141 (measured from Euston via the Trent Valley), between Standon Bridge and Norton Bridge, there were some goods sidings on the down side at Badnall Wharf. Its actual location is in the hamlet of Cold Meece, and from here goods were carted to and from the small town of Eccleshall, 2 miles to the west. This picture shows 'Prince of Wales' 4-6-0 No 5613 *Sydney Smith* coming south on the up fast line on 19 August 1933 while a down goods is receding northwards on the slow. During the Second World War the pleasant countryside on the right of this picture was transformed into sidings to serve the new Royal Ordnance Factory at Swynnerton. After the ROF was closed some of the sidings remained until July 1965, and became well known to enthusiasts as condemned locomotives from all over the former LMS system were concentrated here pending removal to Crewe Works for cutting up

There is now no trace of the sidings or signal box. However, out of the picture on the left the LNWR-built cottages remain in use and the site of the goods yard is used by railway contractors as a land base. Central Trains DMU No 170398 passes by on the up fast working as the 14.40 Liverpool to Birmingham service on 6 April 2005. *E. R. Morten, Martin Welch collection/HB*

NORTON BRIDGE is the junction for the former NSR line to Stone and Stoke-on-Trent, opened in 1848, which curves away north-eastwards behind the signal box in the background. This was the second station in this small village; the first, nearer the actual junction, was closed in 1876 and moved to this location. In this 2 August 1937 picture, which epitomises the high water mark of the British railway network of full facilities, staffed stations and tidy infrastructure, Class 4P Compound No 1166 is arriving at the station from the north with a local train to Stafford. To the left, a 'Royal Scot' stands at the platform facing adverse signals. The railway cottages behind this locomotive remain in occupation today. *E. R. Morten, Martin Welch collection*

NORTON BRIDGE: Seventeen years later, on 3 July 1954, Mr Morten turned around on the station footbridge to photograph 'Jubilee' Class 5XP No 45642 *Boscawen* coming into the station with a northbound local train routed for the Stoke line. In the background an up express with a matching rake of red/cream-liveried stock is heading south.

It is now impossible to repeat the scene as Network Rail made a pre-emptive move and demolished the footbridge in 2004. This appears to have been a determined and surreptitious means of forcing closure of the station following a spurious excuse by Central Trains that the local train service between Stafford and Stoke would be 'temporarily' withdrawn due to staff shortages while people were trained to operate new stock being introduced on its network. Consequently, this picture is taken as close as one can get to the former entrance to the footbridge, and shows Virgin Trains 'Voyager' No 220007 working the 14.48 Birmingham to Manchester service on 13 April 2005. The south-end ramp of the now inaccessible platform is just visible on the extreme left. *E. R. Morten, Martin Welch collection/HB*

GREAT BRIDGEFORD: South of Norton Bridge the Meece Brook and the River Sow join to become a tributary of the Trent, and the railway enters a more open area on reaching Great Bridgeford station, 3½ miles north of Stafford. As with the other stations from Crewe, this also had four platforms, and on a dull August day in 1949 a Fowler Class 4P 2-6-4T pulls out of the station with an up local train.

Although the alignment of the four running lines remains the same, there is no trace of the station platforms or buildings on 1 April 2005. The site of the former goods yard on the right is now a railway contractor's land site and a temporary vehicle access has been made on the left adjacent to the fast lines, behind which the River Sow can be seen. A Central Trains Class 156 DMU is heading south with a Liverpool to Birmingham service. *John K. Williams collection/HB*

STAFFORD: On the approach to Stafford there is much of interest to be seen in this picture of Hughes/Fowler Class 5F 2-6-0 No 42822 (one of five of the class fitted with the Reidlinger version of a rotary cam poppet valve-gear) bringing a train of empty wagons past the junction of two lines off the main line in about 1961. Out of the picture to the left was W. G. Bagnall's locomotive works, with part of its access siding visible, then the two lines curving away formed the Shropshire Union Railways & Canal Company route to Wellington. This railway was leased to the LNWR and opened in 1849, but remained independent until the Grouping on 1 January 1923, when it came into the LMS camp. The line was closed in 1966. Behind the leading brake-van the railway curving to the right was the outpost of the former Great Northern Railway, later LNER, branch from Uttoxeter. This line was opened as the Stafford & Uttoxeter Railway in 1867 and absorbed into the GNR in 1881 (see page 94). As a result of this, local enthusiasts enjoyed the sight of a few GNR/LNER locomotives coming into Stafford. Also behind the train was the extensive and well-known Venables timber yard.

At the same location, seen on 9 April 2005 through a maze of overhead electrification supports, a Virgin Trains 'Pendolino' approaches forming the 13.18 Liverpool to Euston service. Only one truncated track remains on the old Wellington line, disused, and the Uttoxeter route has vanished, as has Venables timber yard, now redeveloped as a housing estate. *John B. Bucknall/HB*

STAFFORD: Looking south from the same bridge, Stafford station can be seen as well-cleaned 'Converted Royal Scot' Class 6P No 46131 *The Royal Warwickshire Regiment* draws out of platform 3 with a Euston to Glasgow train in about 1960. The driver is keeping a sharp lookout as the train eases onto the down fast line. In the background the trainshed covers the main up platform, and the Uttoxeter bay is prominent to the left. On the extreme right part of Stafford No 5 signal box is visible.

The rebuilt station is not readily visible in the present-day picture, but on the skyline it can be seen that the Victorian building has been replaced by a ghastly 1960s concrete slab – of course, a government office! The bay platform for the Uttoxeter trains has also lost its tracks. Stafford No 5 signal box is still in use as Virgin Trains 'Pendolino' No 390048 comes onto the down fast line with the 11.18 Euston to Liverpool service on 1 April 2005. *John B. Bucknall/HB*

STAFFORD SHED: This general view of the shed yard, looking north in about 1963, shows the coaling plant with the ash disposal behind it; part of the shed building can be seen on the extreme left. The first shed was erected by the LNWR in 1852, but in 1860, when the LNWR made Stafford the boundary between its Northern and Southern Divisions, a second shed was built. The depot was coded 5C by the LMS from 1935, in 1937/38 the No 1 shed was demolished, and in 1947 the worn-out roof of the remaining No 2 shed, just visible on the extreme left, was renewed. The shed was finally closed on 19 July 1965. By the coaling stage are Stanier 2-6-4T No 42544 and BR Standard Class 9F No 92026, one of the batch originally fitted with a Crosti boiler.

The whole of the shed yard and its equipment has gone, but the shed building survives in use and is divided into industrial units, part of which is visible on the left, while a new building, also divided into units, stands on the site of the coaling stage and shed yard on 1 April 2005. *John B. Bucknall/HB*

STAFFORD SHED: These pictures show three generations of locomotives seen or stabled at Stafford. In the first, one of the most illustrious of LNWR locomotives stands at Stafford in about 1930, about to pilot a northbound train. Easily distinguished by its impressive nameplate is 'Claughton' No 5964 *Patriot: In Memory of the Fallen L&NWR Employees 1914-1919*, which became a fitting railway war memorial. This engine was built at Crewe in 1920 as No 1914, renumbered 5964 by the LMS in 1926, as seen here, and withdrawn in 1934. In 1937 the LMS transferred the name to 'Patriot' Class 5XP No 5500, which it carried until withdrawal in 1961.

The second picture, taken in low afternoon sunlight, shows the neat lines of one of the 191 'Jubilee' Class 5XP designed by Stanier. Here No 45571 *South Africa* stands in the shed yard in about 1960, quite clean in its BR lined green livery. This engine was built by North British in 1934, named in 1936, and withdrawn in 1964.

In more recent times, following years of embarrassing delays on the line due to locomotive or equipment failures, standby or 'Thunderbird' locomotives are now kept in readiness at various strategic points on the system. At Stafford the standby engine is stabled in the up bay platform, and on 2 April 2005 Class 47 No 47851 *Traction Magazine*, painted in a near copy of its original two-tone green livery, was on duty. *C. L. Hodgetts, John B. Bucknall collection/ John B. Bucknall/HB*

STAFFORD: This good track-level view of Stafford station, taken from the shed yard, shows 'Peak' Class D4 *Great Gable*, in original green livery, passing through the station on the down fast line in about 1960. Behind the train is the trainshed on the up side, and to the right the trainshed and substantial awning covering the down platforms and north-end bays. Behind the locomotive the roof of the Station Hotel can be seen, and to the left the sidings of the Uttoxeter bay platform.

The 'present' picture had to be taken from a slightly more acute angle, but shows the northern ends of the main line platforms, although platforms 5 and 6 are out of sight to the right. Virgin Trains 'Pendolino' No 390039 is leaving platform 3 with the 13.18 Euston to Liverpool service on 2 April 2005. To the left the terraced houses mostly remain, more colourfully presented, but the Station Hotel has gone and the ugly office block has appeared in the background. Likewise, the Uttoxeter bay platform has been converted into part of the station car park, and no doubt now produces much more revenue at £5 a day for parking than that obtained from local train fares. *John B. Bucknall/HB*

STAFFORD: Looking north from the up side, spotless 'Royal Scot' Class 6P No 6166 *London Rifle Brigade* is approaching the station non-stop on the up fast line with 'The Mancunian' from Manchester (London Road) to Euston on 16 March 1933. To the left the old Stafford No 1 loco shed is clearly visible, and to the right is the trackwork leading into the Uttoxeter bay platform. Lower-quadrant LNWR-style signals continue to dominate the scene, and Stafford No 5 signal box is visible behind the engine shunting on the right.

The present-day scene shows a Virgin Trains 'Pendolino' passing on the up fast line forming the 07.38 Glasgow to Euston service on 8 April 2005, with the significant changes of the modern railway in signalling and electrification very apparent. On the left the loco shed yard has become a light industrial estate, although the Stafford loco shed building (originally No 2), modernised and re-roofed, remains sectioned into industrial units. *E. R. Morten, Martin Welch collection/HB*

STAFFORD: Looking north from the down side of the station, 'Coronation' Class 7P No 46221 *Queen Elizabeth* approaches on the up fast, non-stop, with the 'Royal Scot' express from Glasgow to Euston in about 1953. Behind the fourth vehicle Stafford No 5 signal box is prominent.

Besides electrification, the other major changes in this view are that Stafford No 5 signal box was re-sited on the down side in 1954, visible on the extreme left, while on the right the Uttoxeter bay tracks have now become part of the station car park. Virgin Trains 'Voyager' No 220030, on the up main line, is working the 14.54 Manchester to Brighton service on 13 April 2005. *Martin Welch collection/HB*

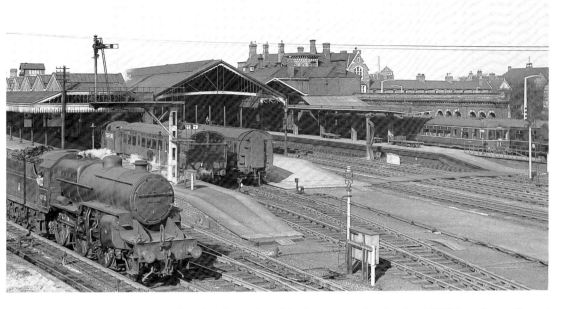

STAFFORD: Moving now to the south end of the station, this picture was taken in about 1960 from the south-west side from the Newport Road bridge not long before demolition and re-building of the station commenced. On the left Hughes/Fowler Class 5F No 42920 is running light engine from the shed yard, and behind it an Ivatt Class 2 2-6-0 stands in one of the bay platforms with an inspection saloon. Across the main running lines a Class 122 DMU in original green livery is in the up bay on a Birmingham service. Note also the LNWR-style water column between the up platform and up main lines, which, no doubt, came in useful to enginemen for topping up while making a booked stop or held by adverse signals on the main line. Standing behind the station is the roof and chimneys of the Station Hotel.

On 13 April 2005 the rebuilt station buildings are nearly lost to view behind the electrification gantries, but the extended platforms are clearly evident. Behind the station the ugly office block has replaced the Station Hotel. *John B. Bucknall/HB*

STAFFORD: This vintage postcard view of the exterior of Stafford station in about 1914 also shows the Station Hotel on the right. This was the third station built by the LNWR and its predecessor the Grand Junction Railway. It was designed by the LNWR architect in an Italianate style and constructed in 1861/62, followed shortly afterwards by the hotel opposite. The hotel had three names during its existence, North Western Railway Hotel, North Western Hotel and finally Station Hotel. Demolition of the station commenced in May 1960 in preparation for rebuilding prior to electrification.

The present station officially opened on 31 December 1962. Like its predecessor it was designed by in-house railway staff, sadly in the austere styling in vogue in the 1950s, with concrete and cheap cladding very evident, no doubt to contain costs. This lack of finish has left the main No 1 up platform with a windswept and gloomy appearance, with old-fashioned lifts for those passengers who cannot use the steep stairs of the overbridge. The vehicle forecourt has recently been redesigned with the 'drop-off' facilities reduced but increased standing for taxis, as seen here. The Station Hotel has been demolished and replaced by the local Mercedes-Benz car dealership, as can be seen on 3 April 2005. *John B. Bucknall collection/HB*

STAFFORD: This busy railway scene is at Queensville curve, where the WCML turns eastwards from Trent Valley Junction, at which point the original Grand Junction line continues south behind Stafford No 1 signal box on the left out of the picture. In about 1960 'Peak' Class D4 *Great Gable* leans into the curve with the up Stranraer to Euston 'Ulster Express', passing 'Jubilee' Class 5XP No 45616 *Malta GC* on the up slow with a mixed goods train. In turn the 'Jubilee' has passed a Stanier Class 8F on a down goods, the engine of which is by the signal box. On the right a made-up ballast train with brake-vans at each end is ready for use, and behind it are the sidings used by Dinham's wagon repair works together with the locomotive water tank and water softening plant.

At least one is still able to take photographs from the footbridge at Queensville, and the WCML retains four tracks. The remnants of the once extensive sidings on the right, disused, are just visible behind Virgin Trains 'Pendolino' No 390045 working the 13.13 Liverpool to Euston service on 1 April 2005. *John B. Bucknall/HB*

Milford Station, STAFFORD

MILFORD & BROCKTON was the first station going south along the Trent Valley line, and was opened in 1877. This circa 1910 postcard view, taken from the down platform, is looking south towards Shugborough Tunnel, through which the four tracks converge to a double line.

No trace of the station remains on 2 April 2005; it was closed in 1950, and track realignment with fast turnouts has taken place so that it is still reduced to a double line before the tunnel. Part of the site of the old goods yard (behind the photographer) is now a railway contractor's road/rail access point. *John K. Williams collection/HB*

SHUGBOROUGH TUNNEL, 777 yards long and 128½ miles from Euston, was built to satisfy Lord Lichfield who lived at Shugborough Hall, in order to preserve the views in his estate. It is in fact the most northerly tunnel on the whole route of 401 miles between Euston and Glasgow. Emerging from the southern end is 'Converted Royal Scot' No 46127 *Old Contemptibles 1914 Aug 5 to Nov 22* running well with an up express in October 1957.

Despite increasing lineside vegetation, using a short telephoto lens the southern portal of Shugborough Tunnel can be photographed from the nearby estate road, and here a Virgin Trains 'Pendolino' is seen working as the 11.15 Liverpool to Euston service on 2 April 2005. *David C. Williams/HB*

COLWICH: These very interesting photographs were taken by a railway civil engineer when infrastructure work prior to electrification was being put in hand at Colwich in February 1961, specifically the reconstruction of bridge No 133 where the railway goes over the road leading to Little Heywood. Two steam cranes were involved: the Rugby crane was a 50-ton Craven RS 1013/50, and somewhat unusually the 45-ton Ransome Rapier crane RS 1097/45 was brought from Wolverhampton Oxley (GWR crane No 17, built in 1940), and they are seen working together adjacent to the old Colwich signal box. The Rugby crane is now preserved on the East Lancashire Railway and the Oxley crane is on the GCR at Loughborough.

The second view is looking the other way towards Stafford, showing the Rugby crane lifting a bridge girder. On the right is part of Colwich signal box, with the road below the bridge, and a Stanier Class 5 behind the crane stands on the direct line to Stoke. No 'day-glo' orange jackets or hard hats on the railwaymen in those days!

The 'present' picture, taken on 2 April 2005, is the nearest angle now possible in order to repeat the first view, and shows bridge No 133 as it is today, just at the point where the North Stafford line from Stoke meets the Trent Valley main line. *Martin Welch (2)/HB*

COLWICH: Coming over the points at the junction of the two lines at Colwich, with bridge No 133 in the foreground, 'Converted Royal Scot' No 64146 *The Rifle Brigade* is heading south with a Euston-bound train in about 1960.

In a similar position on 2 April 2005 a 'Pendolino' is coming over the diamond crossing at Colwich. The trackwork has been simplified and the down Trent Valley line no longer has the point connection prominent in the above scene. The train is the 10.15 Liverpool to Euston service. *Martin Welch/HB*

The junction at Colwich was the scene of a bad accident on 19 September 1985 when No 86429 *The Times* on a down Euston to Manchester via Stoke train and No 86211 *City of Milton Keynes* on an up Liverpool to Euston service collided on the crossing. No 86211 hit the rear cab of No 86429 at speed and both locomotives were severely damaged. Subsequently a small memorial garden was made on the trackside near the signal box with a commemorative plaque and the nameplates of No 86211. This is a very tasteful commemoration, but unfortunately cannot be readily seen by passengers in passing trains unless they are carefully looking for it in advance, as it is very close to the track. Do look out for it when you are next passing. 2 April 2005. *HB*

COLWICH was where the North Staffordshire Railway from Stoke made a connection with the LNWR, and was the most southerly point on the NSR. This undated view, certainly pre-First World War, is looking north towards Stafford and shows that the station only had three platforms, the down on the left and the island platform from which the photograph is taken. The signal box is at the end of the island platform and the junction points for the NSR line, diverging to the right, are just beyond. The station was closed in 1958.

It was impossible to exactly repeat the earlier picture on 2 April 2005 as the photographer would have needed to stand between the fast and slow lines! The wide space between the tracks shows were the island platform was located. The station buildings have gone and their site is now a garage, part of which is on the left in this view. Just left of centre the station master's house remains and is now an attractive private residence. *John K. Williams collection/HB*

COLWICH: This BR official photograph, looking north in about 1961, shows the early stages of the remodelling of the track at Colwich pending electrification. The station buildings have been demolished but the signal box remains in use while new trackwork is in progress.

Today the old signal box has now been replaced with that shown on the right of the 2 April 2005 view, situated on the north side of the railway. *Martin Welch collection/HB*

RUGELEY TRENT VALLEY is seen from the footbridge, looking north, on a rather dull 23 March 1957. The photograph well illustrates the LNWR signal box on the up platform end and sidings on both up and down sides with goods yard on the right.

Today most of the sidings on the up side have been retained for engineering use but the goods yard and signal box have gone, the latter replaced in nearly the same position by a relay cabin, as seen on 24 March 2005. *H. C. Casserley/HB*

RUGELEY TRENT VALLEY: A sight that was once commonplace on the WCML in North Staffordshire was a long mixed goods train hauled by one of the prolific class of LNWR heavy 0-8-0 goods engines. Here, G2a Class 7F No 49377 rumbles past the up platform with a southbound goods train on 9 January 1960.

By the standards of today the WCML sees quite a number of freight trains, but none are conveying goods to local stations. In exactly the same place as the picture above, Direct Rail Services-liveried Class 66/4 No 66402 is seen with train 4M44, the 08.32 Mossend to Daventry Intermodal service, on 24 March 2005. *Michael Mensing/HB*

RUGELEY TRENT VALLEY: This picture, taken from the carriage of a down train on 23 March 1957, shows the substantial awning and buildings on the up platform.

The dire effects of 'rationalisation' of the railway since the 1970s is shown to good effect here, and it is impossible today to visualise that the bleak platform with its tiny 'bus shelter' as the only amenity once looked like the station seen above. The people on the platform on 24 March 2005 are not passengers, but local railway enthusiasts. *R. M. Casserley/HB*

Potteries main line:
Harecastle to Norton Bridge and Colwich

HARECASTLE/KIDSGROVE CENTRAL: The Potteries main line of the North Staffordshire Railway from Stoke to Crewe and Congleton opened in 1848, both of the latter towns being situated in Cheshire. The most northerly station in Staffordshire was the junction at Harecastle, but its opening was delayed until January 1849. This 1964

picture shows the station, renamed Kidsgrove Central in 1944, although later, in 1964, 'Central' was dropped. Coming around the curve from Crewe is Standard Class 9F No 92054 with an up mineral train. The lines to the right are the route to Macclesfield and Manchester. The railway bridge spans the Trent & Mersey Canal, visible bottom right.

Today the station remains open and except for the removal of the signal box and signals the layout is the same. The line to Crewe has now been electrified to complete a useful gap in the 25Kv network. Increasing vegetation is the only thing that diminishes the picture. The rear of the 'Pendolino' seen on the right is heading towards Manchester on 14 April 2005. *Martin Welch/HB*

HARECASTLE TUNNEL: The North Stafford main line was expensive to build, not least due to two viaducts near Congleton, and just south of Harecastle three tunnels. The north tunnel was 130 yards long and this 1965 picture shows Stanier Class 8F No 48353 emerging from the middle tunnel of 180 yards into the deep cutting, before entering the south tunnel, by far the longest at 1,750 yards. On the left are the bracket distant signals giving advance notice of the junction ahead, seen in the previous picture.

When preparations were being made for electrification of the route in the 1960s, it was found that the tunnels were in poor physical condition, necessitating extensive repairs and presenting a serious obstacle to progress.

Therefore the Harecastle diversion, 2 miles 50 yards long, was constructed to bypass the three tunnels on the old line. The abandoned cutting on the old route is quite accessible today and the southern portal of the middle tunnel is visible, though fenced off. On the right of this 4 April 2005 view the low retaining wall is intact. *Martin Welch/HB*

HARECASTLE TUNNEL: Emerging from the south end of the south tunnel is Stanier Class 5 No 44761 with what is thought to be the afternoon Crewe Works to Stoke unadvertised staff train on 19 July 1965.

Taken from the same road overbridge as the 'past' picture, on 4 April 2005, peering through the vegetation the cutting is discernable and the house, top right, can just be glimpsed. *Martin Welch/HB*

HARECASTLE DIVERSION: During the latter stages of completing the new Harecastle diversion in August 1965 the District Engineer has come to inspect the newly laid track, using his saloon hauled by a Stanier Class 5 4-6-0. The Engineer and staff are standing by the south end of the new tunnel, 220 yards long burrowing under a ridge 73 feet high.

The area around and above the tunnel forms a local amenity, but more vegetation is evident together with the ever-increasing steel palisade flanking the railway boundary. A Virgin Trains 'Pendolino' en route to Manchester is disappearing into the tunnel on 4 April 2005. *Martin Welch/HB*

HARECASTLE DIVERSION: On 27 June 1966 the new line, duly electrified, was opened for traffic and five days afterwards, on 2 July, Stanier Class 8F No 48767 is heading south towards Stoke with a Shell oil tank train.

To the author's pleasant surprise when arriving at the footbridge on 4 April 2005 to take the 'present' equivalent he found that the line was readily visible with the tunnel in the background. In 39 years the vegetation has substantially increased but there is an unobstructed view of Virgin Trains 'Pendolino' working as the 12.45 Manchester to Euston service. Today this line rarely sees locomotive-hauled trains, DMUs and EMUs have a complete monopoly of passenger services, and there are no regular booked freight trains. *Martin Welch/HB*

LONGPORT: The first station in the industrial area of the Potteries conurbation that the NSR main line approached from the north was Longport. Very much on its home territory, a former NSR 'L' Class 0-6-2T, now in LMS livery as No 2241, is passing Longport station with a southbound goods train in about 1935. The locomotive was built by Vulcan Foundry in 1903 and withdrawn in 1936.

Longport station is still open as an unstaffed halt, although the very attractive station building, in a Jacobean gabled style, which the NSR used for a number of its stations, is boarded up and minus its chimneys, an inviting target for the vandals in the area. Other changes from the 'past' picture are that the level-crossing has been replaced by a footbridge and the gas-holder and terraced houses have gone. Virgin Trains 'Voyager' No 220021 has passed the station non-stop working as the 11.24 Manchester to Birmingham service on 7 April 2005. *Martin Welch collection/HB*

GRANGE JUNCTION, ETRURIA: With the back-drop of the British Steel Shelton Bar steel works, Class 56 No 56069 *Wolverhampton Steel Terminal*, in Railfreight two-tone grey livery with Railfreight Metals sub-sector symbols, eases pass the junction with train 6E09, the 16.06 Etruria to Tees Yard, conveying steel sections on 17 June 1993.

The steel works at Shelton closed in 2000 and consequently there is no more rail traffic here. Much of the works remains, however, although the buildings to the left have gone, as has Grange Junction signal box. Virgin Trains 'Pendolino' No 390029, appropriately named *City of Stoke-on-Trent*, is working as the 12.45 Manchester to Euston service on 7 April 2005. *Paul D. Shannon/HB*

STOKE-ON-TRENT: The six Pottery Towns (not five as incorrectly made famous by Arnold Bennett) celebrated the Jubilee of the creation of the City of Stoke-on-Trent in 1960, and a railway exhibition was held in the yard on the north side of Stoke station in May of that year. To emphasise the old North Staffordshire Railway, very appropriately the National Coal Board lent its surviving NSR locomotive as a prime exhibit. This engine, originally Class 'New L' 0-6-2T No 2, was built at Stoke in 1923, the first year of the Grouping, but it still appeared in NSR livery of Madder Lake crimson lined in black, yellow and vermilion. The engine became LMS No 2271, and was withdrawn in 1937 and sold to Manchester Collieries to become *Princess*. It was especially repainted in NSR livery for this exhibition.

After the Stoke exhibition the locomotive returned to the NCB at Manchester, but was eventually withdrawn in 1966. Being the only surviving NSR steam locomotive, it was preserved and is now part of the National Collection in the control of the National Railway Museum, York. However, it has spent some years at the Churnet Valley Railway, Cheddleton, but only cosmetically restored and has not been steamed. Recently the NRM recalled the engine for display at its new out-station at Shildon. Here the engine is seen on 31 March 2005 in the shed yard at Cheddleton, on its native railway, the day before it left on a low-loader for County Durham. *John K. Williams/HB*

STOKE-ON-TRENT: In this view looking north from the end of the down platform at Stoke station, there are changes from the scene on page 6. Note that there are fewer sidings by Stoke North signal box and one of the two centre lines through the station has been removed. Also, the University building to the right of the locomotive has been extended. Stanier Class 8F No 48094 is passing a departing northbound DMU as it approaches the station with an up mineral train on 1 May 1965.

All the sidings and the signal box on the left have gone, while to the right of the train the car parking area is prominent. Virgin Trains 'Pendolino' No 390046 arrives as the 13.15 Manchester to Euston service on 7 April 2005; behind the third coach is Stoke power-box. *Martin Welch/HB*

STOKE-ON-TRENT: This well-known but fine turn-of-the-19th-century scene of the up platform at Stoke shows NSR Class 'L' 0-6-2T No 167 (built by Vulcan Foundry in 1893 and withdrawn as LMS No 2244 in 1935) passing the platform with a southbound goods train. Note the NSR 'Knotty' emblem on the back of the barrow in the right foreground.

This 'present' picture had to be taken a little further along the platform, as the 'past' spot was blocked by substantial scaffolding for roof maintenance, but fortunately the pleasing features of this impressive station, not least the overall roof, have been retained. The station was opened in 1848 and was the headquarters and focal point of the NSR. On the right the archway over the exit was erected and unveiled in August 1922 as a fitting memorial to the 'Knotty' railwaymen killed in the First World War. On the left of this 7 April 2005 view Class 66 No 66177 is on a trip working with one wagon to the Marcroft Wagon Repair Works located a mile to the south of the station. *John K. Williams collection/HB*

STOKE-ON-TRENT station is seen again from the up platform in BR steam days. There are two through non-platform lines and Glebe Street signal box is visible on the left. All the buildings behind the train are railway premises, mainly used by the signal engineering department. The approaching train to Llandudno in August 1961 is hauled by modified Stanier Class 5 No 44686, most distinctive with its double chimney, high running plate, Caprotti valve gear and roller bearings.

Today the track has been reduced to one centre through line, the signal box has gone, and the former railway buildings behind the platform on the right have been sold out of railway use. Local enthusiast John Steele obligingly stands in a similar position to the man in the 'past' picture and watches Virgin Trains 'Pendolino' No 390002 arriving with the 09.05 Euston to Manchester service on 7 April 2005. *Martin Welch/HB*

STOKE-ON-TRENT: The south end of the station is seen from the down platform on 1 May 1965, prior to electrification, but in anticipation thereof one of the two centre lines has already been removed. The three-car DMU is pulling out of the station while a Stanier Class 8F appears to be coming slowly under the roof towards an adverse signal protecting the DMU in front of it.

On 12 April 2005, except for the 25kv overhead wires and supports the scene has hardly changed in 40 years. If anything there is an improvement: the glazing in the station roof is in much better condition, as the whole area was repainted and tidied up several years ago. The same cannot be said for the grubby-looking Class 87, No 87014, a southbound light engine, now devoid of its nameplates and Virgin insignia. *Martin Welch/HB*

STOKE-ON-TRENT SHED: Another well-known historic NSR photograph, the first picture shows the straight shed at Stoke erected in the 1870s opposite the original roundhouse and locomotive works, which were situated on the west side of the main line to Colwich. This shed comprised two hipped-roof sections of slated timber covering three roads each. Later a single-road extension was built on the north side, seen here to the left in about 1910. Notice the remarkable cleanliness of the shed yard and the spotless condition of the four engines – left to right, they are Class 'G' 4-4-0 No 87 (built at Stoke in 1910 and withdrawn in 1929), a Class 'D' 0-6-0T (built Stoke 1907, withdrawn 1937), Class 'M' 0-4-4T No 9 (built Stoke 1907, withdrawn 1936), and 0-6-2T Class 'New L' No 93 (built Stoke 1909, withdrawn 1934).

Much-needed improvements to the shed were partially carried out until interrupted by the Second World War. The intention was to re-roof the shed, but by September 1939 only the northern half had been completed, while the other half of the hipped roof was never replaced, as seen here in about 1960. However, due to the latter's poor condition it was removed a few years before closure, leaving the shed open to the elements. On the left is the coaler and ash disposal plant built in 1936. The coaler had a capacity of 150 tons with twin feeds. The picture shows Class 4F No 44315 and Class 5 No 45357 on the left, with other Stanier and Fowler engines outside the shed. Stoke shed was coded 5D in the LMS coding of 1935 and was closed to steam on 7 August 1967.

It is impossible today to stand in the same position; indeed, there is no trace whatsoever of this large shed. This picture was taken on 12 April 2005 looking across the dormant track of the branch to Leek Brook Junction from the car park of a tile warehouse, and shows the site to be just waste ground with trees and scrub well in command. *Martin Welch collection/ Martin Welch/HB*

TRENTHAM was the next station coming south from Stoke; it was the nearest station on the main line to Trentham Hall, seat of the Duke of Sutherland, and was built in an Italianate style with an ornate pantile roof, part of which can be seen here. Well-cleaned Class 4F 0-6-0 No 4311 comes south with a goods train in this undated scene, but thought to be about 1926. In the background are colliery sidings that connected with the Florence Colliery Railway and, later, a new coal mine at Hem Heath.

There is no trace of the station as Virgin Trains 'Pendolino' speeds by as the 09.45 Manchester to Euston service on 4 April 2005. To the right of the train the head-shunt of the former sidings serving Hem Heath colliery remains disused as the colliery, the last working in North Staffordshire, has closed. In the background, behind the ever-encroaching vegetation, part of the Britannia football stadium can be seen. *John K. Williams collection/HB*

TRENTHAM PARK: The short branch from Trentham to Trentham Park, just 1 mile 14 chains long, was the last branch opened by the NSR, on 1 April 1910. Trentham was developing as a suburb of Stoke and there was the local attraction of Trentham Hall with its large deer park and gardens. By this time the Duke of Sutherland had ceased to use the Hall as one of his residences due, it is said, 'to the pestilential odour of the nearby River Trent, which has been made noxious by its pollution through the Pottery towns'. Even so, the Potteries people, and others who came by excursion trains, enjoyed the amenities of the gardens and today it continues as a garden centre and conference hall. There had been plans to extend the branch towards Pool Dam in Newcastle-under-Lyme and Silverdale, but this was delayed by the First World War and afterwards road transport began to erode the local traffic, so this was never implemented. In 1946 the station was renamed Trentham Gardens and the branch was closed to all traffic on 1 October 1957. After closure the Stephenson Locomotive Society ran this special over the branch on 31 May 1958, seen at Trentham Gardens hauled by Class 4P 2-6-4T No 42482.

Except for a small piece of brick wall at the bottom of the station road leading up from the A34, this 4 April 2005 view shows that all traces of the railway have been obliterated by housing development. An elderly resident in the neighbourhood helpfully stated that the engine in the 'past' picture would be standing near the right-hand end of the concrete boundary wall inside the gate of the house on the right. *R. M. Casserley/HB*

BARLASTON & TITTENSOR: Back on the main line coming south, a station was opened here in 1850, but in 1972 it was simply renamed Barlaston by BR, logical because it is situated in that village. The platforms are immediately north of a level-crossing, with the signal box and goods yard to the south. This undated view from about 1960, looking north, shows the small signal box, crossing, station building on the right and the two platforms.

The 31 March 2005 view shows that the siding, signal box and station building have gone and the level-crossing gates have been replaced by automatic barriers. Although nominally open at the time of writing, no trains stop here as the service has been 'temporary suspended' by Central Trains, allegedly due to 'shortage of drivers because of training on other units'. Many local people are suspicious that this is leading to closure by stealth, but so far no further information is forthcoming. *John K. Williams collection/HB*

STONE station, serving the market town on the main NSR route to Norton Bridge, opened on 1 April 1848 and a year later the company extended the railway south to Colwich, thus making it a junction station. The station building, in the vee of the diverging lines, is an impressive building designed by Sir Henry Arthur Hunt in the NSR Jacobean style with gables. The Norton Bridge lines are to the left, those to Colwich to the right, and the goods shed is visible behind. The picture is undated, but from the Staffordshire-registered Wolseley car on the right it could be about 1957.

The station was unmanned for some years but fortunately was not demolished, and in 2003 extensive refurbishment was undertaken by Stone Town Council for community use, with funds obtained from the Heritage Lottery Fund, Railway Heritage Trust and Onyx Environmental Trust. This project resulted in the Town Council receiving a National Railway Heritage Award and the 'Modern Railways' Restoration Award, presented by the Duke of Gloucester in 2004. This is the building on 31 March 2005. *John K. Williams collection/HB*

STONE: The line to Norton Bridge makes a sharp curve through the station, and two-car Class 127 parcels DMU Nos 55972 and 55982 slowly passes the platform as a Manchester to Birmingham parcels working on 29 September 1987. These parcel units were painted dark blue with an orange band edged in yellow; the seats inside were removed and a roller shutter door fitted midway along the side.

The extensive refurbishment of the station can be seen here with new platform edging and footbridge as Virgin Trains 'Voyager' No 220015 slowly passes with the 11.54 Manchester to Birmingham service on 31 March 2005. *Both HB*

COLD MEECE BRANCH: A little-known branch was constructed by the LMS during the Second World War, and opened on 5 August 1941 to provide a station for the workers at the large Royal Ordnance Factory No 5 near Swynnerton, tucked out of the way in the rolling North Staffordshire countryside, 4 miles west of Stone. The branch left the Stone to Norton Bridge line at Swynnerton Junction and ran for 1½ miles to a four-platform basic brick-built station in the hamlet of Cold Meece. The branch never appeared in the public timetables, but when production at the ROF got into full swing by June 1942 more than 8,000 passengers used the station every day with trains coming from all parts of the Potteries. It was also used by thousands of American personnel travelling to a nearby base. This 28 February 1958 picture, looking towards the buffers, shows the simple layout with the island platform flanked by two outer platforms and engine run-round roads in between the platform lines.

On the same day Stanier Class 4P 2-6-4T No 42665 starts away from platform 2 with a workers train to Silverdale. Note the leaking steam from the carriage heating pipes.

The station was closed on 26 June 1958 and the site is now a government Goods Vehicle Testing Station. There is no trace of the railway at all, and the only way to approximate the 'past' picture was to try and line up the trees in the background. This view shows the staff and visitors' car park on 31 March 2005; the actual vehicle testing building is behind the hedge on the left. *H. B. Oliver, R. M. Casserley collection (2)/HB*

COLD MEECE BRANCH: On a bright winter's afternoon, thought to be in 1943, a Stanier 2-6-4T engine has just arrived at platform 1 and the train is disgorging a huge crowd of workers, all quickly making for the exit and the nearby ROF. When shown to the author's wife, she commented how slim the mainly female passengers appeared, all wearing skirts and coats and looking cheerful, considering the dangerous work of filling bomb and shell casings many of them were going to do. Notice also that the few men in the picture are more elderly. *R. M. Casserley collection*

SANDON: Back on the NSR, south from Stone the railway, which closely follows the River Trent to Colwich, was opened in 1849. At Sandon, no doubt influenced by the nearby Sandon Hall, another most attractive station in the favoured Jacobean style with gables and patterned brickwork was built. This undated postcard view of about 1910 is looking north towards Stone.

It was very pleasing to find on 24 March 2005 that this beautiful building still survives and is now a private house. The station was closed to passengers on 6 January 1947 and to goods on 5 September 1955. The platforms and goods yard have gone and a relay box has been built in part of the yard; likewise a small extension to the house now protrudes over what had been part of the platform. *John K. Williams collection/HB*

WESTON & INGESTRE was the next station south, and this view shows the layout looking south in 1951, four years after the station was closed to passengers. However, the goods yard survived until 2 September 1963 and some wagons can just be seen adjacent to the substantial goods shed. 1951.

The only evidence that a station may have existed here is the old station approach road on the right, otherwise on 24 March 2005 nothing remains and the former goods yard is now occupied by a caravan dealer. *R. M. Casserley collection/HB*

Potteries loop line

KIDSGROVE LIVERPOOL ROAD was the most northerly station on the Potteries Loop, which was opened in stages; this was the last part to open, in 1875. By the time this picture was taken on 26 September 1960 the station was looking very run-down, and the train has just completed a convoluted movement, having come from Crewe. Stanier Class 4 2-6-4T No 42668 heads the 4.26pm empty stock working from Crewe, which will form a workers' train from the Royal Ordnance Factory at Radway Green to Stoke. This meant that at Kidsgrove Central the train had to reverse on to the Macclesfield line, then run forward again into this station. The signal box in the background on the main line is Kidsgrove Junction.

The station site has now become a Tesco supermarket and the platforms part of the car park. The points of reference on 25 March 2005 are the houses on the right, and in the background behind the steel fence the 25Kv overhead equipment on the main line to Macclesfield can be seen. *Michael Mensing/HB*

KIDSGROVE MARKET STREET HALT: Fowler Class 4P 2-6-4T No 42343 makes an impressive sight on the 1 in 40 climb from Kidsgrove towards the Loop Line summit near Newchapel & Goldenhill with the Manchester University Railway Society's 'The Staffordshire Potter' special from Manchester Ancoats Goods to various lines in the area on 13 March 1965. The halt had been closed on 25 September 1950.

The location has been tidied up and the railway cutting partially filled in, while to the left a footpath and grassed area has been formed. There has also been redevelopment to many of the roads around Kinnersley Street in the background, but the house on the extreme right in both pictures remains substantially the same on 25 March 2005. *Gavin Morrison/HB*

NEWCHAPEL & GOLDENHILL was just to the south of the Loop Line summit, and this 12 April 1962 picture is looking south two years before the station was closed to passengers on 2 March 1964.

Much of the trackbed of the Loop Line has been converted into a cycle/walkway and on 25 March 2005 the pathway is being surfaced. The path also goes under the overbridge from which the two photographs have been taken. The only evidence of the station is the platform edging on the right-hand side. *F. W. Shuttleworth, John K. Williams collection/HB*

NEWFIELDS BRANCH was a short 1-mile-long goods-only line off the Loop Line at Newfields Junction. Despite its short distance it necessitated a reversal near the junction, followed by a ferocious climb, partly at 1 in 37, up to Newfields Wharf, seen here. The branch was the preserve of LNWR 'Cauliflower' 0-6-0s, two being allocated to Stoke shed for this job, and one of which, No 58382, is seen shunting in the yard on 29 June 1953. The branch was closed on 3 August 1959.

The railway wharf has been replaced by a light industrial estate with alterations in the levels. The overbridge from which the 'past' picture was taken has been filled in and this scene is just inside the revised level at the rear of AVC Woodworkers' premises, looking in the same direction. The houses in Adams Avenue on the left can still just be seen in this 25 March 2005 view. *F. W. Shuttleworth, John K. Williams collection/HB*

TUNSTALL was one of four of the 'Six Towns' served by the Loop Line, and here we see a three-car Class 104 DMU at the station forming the 5.25pm service from Manchester to Stoke-on-Trent on 28 September 1963.

All trace of the station has gone and the trackbed forms part of the 'Burslem Greenway', with a pedestrian tunnel taking the path northwards under the former road overbridge. The station master's house, seen in the 'past' picture above the front of the DMU, survives on 14 April 2005 as a private residence. In a quite incongruous position, presumably as a reminder that a railway once existed here, a rusty signal post with home and distant arms stands forlornly by the walkway. *Michael Mensing/HB*

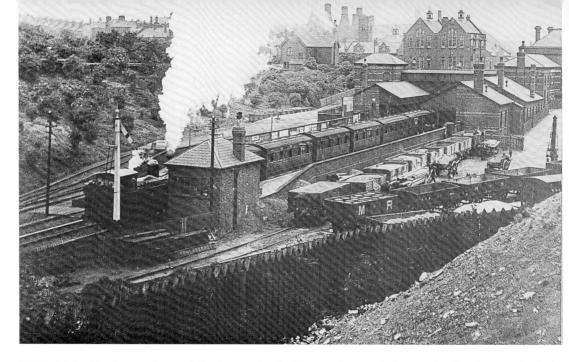

BURSLEM: In this vintage picture of Burslem station looking south towards Stoke, a local train comprised of a mixed rake of coaches is passing the signal box travelling north towards Tunstall in about 1914. There is much activity in the goods yard, behind which the substantial main station building can be seen together with Moorland Road bridge over the railway. In the background some of the distinctive 'pot-banks' are visible, as Burslem was a major pottery-producing town, as well as Moorland Road School, erected in 1910. As with the other stations on the Loop Line, passenger trains were withdrawn on 2 March 1964, but goods facilities lingered on until 3 January 1966.

On 25 March 2005 all trace of the railway has gone, substituted by the walkway running down the centre of the cutting in which the railway had been situated, and the site landscaped and now included as a continuation of the adjacent, and most attractive, Burslem Park, out of the picture on the left. In the background the 'pot-banks' have gone and Moorland Road School has now been reduced in size and become the New Burslem Enterprise Centre. *John K. Williams collection/HB*

COBRIDGE station is seen here looking north towards Burslem on a wet and gloomy 10 April 1955, with the signals 'off' for a down train. In the murk beyond the signal Cobridge signal box can be just made out. Behind the photographer the railway entered Cobridge Tunnel, 310 yards long descending at 1 in 67 towards Hanley.

On 25 March 2005 the wall bounding the former path down to the up platform still provides access to what in this area is called the Forest Park Walkway. No other trace of the railway remains and the tunnel is now filled in at this end. *John K. Williams/HB*

HANLEY station was in the commercial centre of the Potteries and the City of Stoke-on-Trent, and although conveniently located it was in a very restricted position. The platforms were in a deep cutting with vertical retaining walls, and on a sharp curve of 8 chains radius, necessitating check-rails. This view is looking towards Etruria in August 1957.

The cutting has been filled in and the station buildings at street level demolished; the only evidence that a railway once existed here is the top of the road bridge seen in the background of the 'past' picture opposite. The levelled area is now part of the car park for the Quality Hotel, out of the picture on the left of this 27 March 2005 view. *John K. Williams collection/HB*

HANLEY: A three-car Class 104 DMU leaves Hanley as the 1.55pm Macclesfield to Stoke service on 28 September 1963. Again this picture well emphasises the tight location and sharp curve of the station and track. The station building is on the right at street level behind the road overbridge.

Not only has the cutting been filled in but the station and the former buildings on both sides have also gone, leaving no trace of the railway other than the top of the road overbridge. This view is looking north on 27 March 2005, with the Quality Hotel on the extreme right of the picture. *Michael Mensing/HB*

ETRURIA JUNCTION: Another three-car Class 104 DMU, forming the 4.42pm Wolverhampton to Manchester service, is starting its journey up the Loop Line on 28 September 1963 and is seen between Etruria Junction and Hanley, about to pass under the Etruria Road bridge. Behind the train are Shelton Colliery Sidings and part of the extensive Shelton steel works at Etruria.

Looking in the same direction today, no one would believe that a railway or steel works ever existed in the area. Following closure of the steel works and railway the whole district was redeveloped with road improvements and complete landscaping prior to the City of Stoke-on-Trent hosting the 1986 National Garden Festival. Following the Garden Festival a shopping complex and leisure facilities in what became the Festival Park have been provided. The photographer was able to locate the 'past' view because behind him the area has not been much altered and the trackbed is readily discernable, even though the road levels have changed. On 27 March 2005 the flyover bridge of the A53 road to Leek dominates and the building behind, which could be mistaken for being part of the steel works, is in fact the side of the Odeon cinema in the Festival Park! *Michael Mensing/HB*

ETRURIA JUNCTION: In this panoramic view looking north at Etruria Junction on 16 July 1964, Fowler Class 3F 0-6-0T No 47546, hauling a long rake of wagons, passes the point where the Loop Line joined the main line. By the time of this picture the passenger train service over the Loop had been withdrawn and the junction connection reduced to a single line. The main Potteries line and Etruria down yard is to the left, and in the far left background the then modern Wolstanton Colliery is visible. In the centre are the extensive sidings comprising Grange and Etruria yards, full of wagons, and in the right background are the blast furnaces of the steel works in Etruria.

The 'present' picture is a stark and depressing reminder that the whole industrial base upon which the Potteries was founded has disappeared. Etruria is no longer a junction, Wolstanton Colliery, Shelton steel works and blast furnaces, and most of the railway sidings have gone, and those that remain are currently out of use. Virgin Trains 'Voyager' DMU No 221122 is working the 13.45 Manchester to Birmingham service on 27 March 2005. *R. H. Brough, Martin Welch collection/HB*

Newcastle Junction to Silverdale

NEWCASTLE JUNCTION, just north of Stoke-on-Trent station, was where the NSR line turned westwards to Newcastle-under-Lyme, ultimately connecting with the Great Western Railway at Market Drayton in Shropshire. Here Stanier Class 8F 2-8-0 No 48291 passes the Junction signal box with an up ballast train on 12 March 1965. To the right, the Trent & Mersey Canal is visible.

The junction here was finally severed when the remnant of the branch to Brampton Sidings was closed on 8 March 1966 prior to electrification of the main line to Stockport. Now the railway is much reduced as Virgin Trains 'Voyager' No 221115 approaches Stoke with a Manchester to Birmingham service on 15 May 2005. *R. H. Brough, Martin Welch collection/HB*

NEWCASTLE-UNDER-LYME is a large town adjacent to, but not part of, the Pottery towns or the City of Stoke-on-Trent. The station, in King Street, was fairly convenient for the town centre and this picture is looking west at the Queen Street road overbridge in the direction of Silverdale, in about 1910. Opened on 6 September 1852, the station was closed to passengers on 2 March 1964.

There is no trace of the station on 27 March 2005, and only a raised grassed area above the level of the original formation and a pedestrian tunnel, full of water when inspected on the date of this photograph, under the road bridge in the 'past' picture, indicates that a railway once served the area. *John K. Williams collection/HB*

LIVERPOOL ROAD HALT: The west side of Newcastle-under-Lyme was served by four halts all within 2 miles before the next station at Silverdale was reached. This is the second halt from Newcastle-under-Lyme, looking towards Market Drayton from a Stoke-bound train on 28 August 1954. The very short platform is adjacent to the main road overbridge of the same name.

The grass walkway from Newcastle-under-Lyme continues west past the site of the Halt and another pedestrian tunnel under Liverpool Road, with no trace of the railway on 27 March 2005. *R. M. Casserley/HB*

SILVERDALE: In 1962 the Madeley Chord was opened to provide a connection with the Market Drayton branch from the West Coast Main Line in order that 'merry-go-round' coal trains could run to and from what were then still productive collieries at Silverdale and nearby Holditch. Looking west towards the chord line and the remains of the disused station at Silverdale, a loading hopper has been constructed over the up line and the down track slewed around it. Class 60 No 60047 *Robert Owen* is running round its incoming train of empties before loading up with coal for Fiddlers Ferry power station on 19 June 1993.

Once the mines in the Silverdale area ceased production there was no longer any use for the chord line and today it is dormant. As seen on 27 March 2005, both the derelict station building and the loading hopper have been demolished; likewise, all the nearby colliery buildings out of the picture to the right have been removed. *Paul D. Shannon/HB*

SILVERDALE: In this general view of the station and goods yard looking east in about 1905, the spire of St Luke the Evangelist Church is prominent behind the goods shed. To the left of the station there was a level-crossing rather the footbridge later substituted when the road was diverted.

Due to the proximity of the old Silverdale Colliery site on the north side of the railway, and subsequent landscaping, it was impossible to exactly repeat the 'past' location on 27 March 2005. This view is nearer the station site and further back from the line due to the colliery road in the foreground, but it shows that the wall at the back of the down platform remains. The goods yard is now just waste ground and substantially overgrown with scrub. *John K. Williams collection/HB*

Biddulph Valley line to Stoke Junction and Leek Brook Junction

BLACK BULL: Coming south on the Biddulph Valley line from Congleton to Milton Junction on a dull 13 March 1965, Fowler Class 4P 2-6-4T No 42343 passes Black Bull signal box with 'The Staffordshire Potter' (see page 62). This area was once heavily industrialised with collieries, ironworks and a connection with Heath's Railway, a private mineral railway that connected with his Birchenwood Colliery and coke works near Kidsgrove.

It is quite impossible now to realise that vast heavy industries with supporting railways once existed in this region south of Biddulph, as all visual signs of activity have gone and landscaping of the area has completely changed it out of all recognition. The author was able to work out the alignment of the railway in the 'past' picture as there were traces of the overbridge on the Brindley Ford to Packmoor minor road to provide a bearing on 26 March 2005. *Gavin Morrison/HB*

FORD GREEN: The Biddulph Valley line was closed to passenger traffic on 11 July 1927, and this picture, taken in August 1958, 31 years after closure, shows the station master's house and platform at Ford Green in a very neat and tidy condition. The picture was taken from the road overbridge looking south towards Milton Junction.

Goods traffic on this line ceased in 1977, and the trackbed now forms part of the 'Whitfield Valley Greenway'; the road overbridge has been removed so this 26 March 2005 picture had to be taken at ground level. Part of the brick wall under the white fence in the 'past' picture remains, and the railway house continues to be lived in.
R. M. Casserley collection/HB

MILTON JUNCTION: Looking north on 11 April 1986, the Biddulph Valley line passed to the left of the signal box, but this train is coming south towards Stoke from Leek Brook Junction. Taken in the period when the location had been reduced to basic operating level by BR, Class 25 No 25205 stands by the box with train 7G42, the 12.55 Oakamoor to Witton sand train.

The signal box at Milton Junction has gone but one line seen here on 23 March 2005, to Leek Brook Junction, remains dormant. Out of the picture to the left, the trackbed of the Biddulph Valley line is at this point used as an unofficial footpath, mainly by dog-walkers. The building above the Class 25 in the 'past' picture is now part of 'Mr Lucky Bags' factory – makers of sweets and bags for children. *Paul D. Shannon/HB*

FENTON MANOR was the only station south from Milton Junction before the Biddulph Valley and Leek Brook Junction lines met the NSR main line at Stoke Junction. Looking north, the up distant signal on the right was in advance of Stoke Junction. In the background is one of many colliery waste tips, a once prolific sight in the Potteries. This picture was taken on 2 April 1956, one month before the station was closed to passengers.

Vegetation has increased, but the down line remains in situ on 12 April 2005, albeit disused. The platform edges are still visible and the house, top right in both pictures, is now an office. The large waste tip has been removed.
F. W. Shuttleworth, V. & R. Anderson collection/HB

ENDON: The line towards Leek from Milton Junction was opened three years after the Biddulph Valley railway, on 1 November 1867. This is Endon station, looking east on 25 June 1972 after the station was closed to both passenger and goods traffic but with the line still open for freight to the Caldon Low quarries and sand quarry near Oakamoor until 1988.

The station building at Endon remains in commercial use, but the up line, signal box and level-crossing gates have gone. The latter have been replaced with flashing warning lights, but as the line is dormant the local vandals presumably considered it their prerogative to vandalise them. Standing at the platform on the down line on 12 April 2005 is a road/rail machine, which was apparently being used for some vegetation clearance. *J. A. Sommerfield, John K. Williams collection/HB*

WALL GRANGE & LONGSDON was an attractive station, and is seen here on 29 June 1953 with a down train to Leek at the platform. The water tower on the skyline belongs to the County Mental Hospital at Cheddleton. The station was closed to passengers on 7 May 1956.

On 30 May 1964 the Railway Correspondence & Travel Society ran its 'North Staffordshire Rail Tour' from Birmingham to the Stoke area; hauled by Stanier Class 5 No 45020, the train is seen passing Wall Grange & Longsdon on its way back to Stoke from Leek Brook Junction.

On 23 March 2005, although the station buildings have gone, the up platform survives and the station master's house remains as a residence in this very peaceful and attractive location. The down line is out of use and the water tower in the background of the former mental hospital still overlooks the scene. *F. W. Shuttleworth, John K. Williams collection/ Michael Mensing/ HB*

LEEK BROOK JUNCTION, south of Leek, had lines radiating to all four points of the compass, and here a train is crossing east to west over the north-south Churnet Valley line, just visible behind the signal box. Class 40 No 40174 eases very slowly around the sharp curve on to the Stoke line with 7L82, a Caldon to Witton stone train, on 10 April 1984.

The signal box, although boarded up out of use, is now owned by the Churnet Valley Railway, hence its position on the far side of Network Rail's steel palisade. Nearer the camera the four tracks seen in the above picture are still in situ, although the two lines on the left are hidden under rapidly growing saplings on 8 April 2005. *Paul D. Shannon/HB*

Leek Brook Junction to Waterhouses and the Leek & Manifold Valley Light Railway

LEEK BROOK JUNCTION: Looking due north towards Leek, this train has come up the Churnet Valley and the locomotives, having run round their train, will now proceed westwards towards Stoke, going to the left out of the picture. Class 25s Nos 25176 and 25210 are hauling a sand train, number 8K02, from Oakamoor to Worksop and St Helens on 10 April 1984

   The track remains in situ at Leek Brook Junction and likewise the stop block and lamp post. The signal was sold to the Churnet Valley Railway and was taken down into their safe custody on 24 March 2005. *Paul D. Shannon/HB*

BRADNOP: This well-known vintage scene shows Bradnop station at about the time of its opening in 1905. The inspection train is being propelled towards Waterhouses by NSR Class 'D' 0-6-0T No 135. The station was situated on the 1 in 40 to 1 in 59 climb all the way from Leek Brook Junction to the branch summit just beyond Ipstones.

Other than the footpath (not visible in the picture) from the main road that runs above and parallel to the railway down to the former platform, and the track itself, on 8 April 2005 there is no evidence that a station existed here. *John K. Williams collection/HB*

CALDON LOW: The hillside and limestone quarry dominate the scene behind the train at Caldon Low as Class 25 No 25176 makes ready to leave with a train to Witton on 22 April 1985.

Surprisingly in this day and age, when politicians talk incessantly about the environment and encouraging rail transport, all the production from this quarry is today sent out by road – hence the view here. The track is still in position but nature is taking over on 8 April 2005. *Paul D. Shannon/HB*

CALDON LOW: Looking west towards Stoke on 30 May 1964, enthusiasts from the RCTS 'North Staffordshire Rail Tour' take in the scene at this remote freight-only branch line, nearly 1,100 feet above sea level in the Staffordshire moorlands. The train engine, Stanier Class 5 No 45020, has already run round the six-coach train prior to returning to Stoke.

In amongst the vegetation on 8 April 2005 the track and weighbridge are almost completely hidden as enthusiast Geoffrey Dingle contemplates why rail-borne traffic has ceased to be sent from this quarry. *R. M. Casserley/HB*

WATERHOUSES was the terminus of the 9¾-mile branch from Leek and the exchange station for the Leek & Manifold Light Railway. This view of 15 September 1930 is looking towards the buffer stops on the standard gauge line with a former NSR 0-6-0T, now LMS No 1597, standing at the platform with a train to Leek. The weather-beaten name-board on the left reads 'Waterhouses for Froghall Quarry', and the station was closed to passengers on 30 September 1935, 18 months after the Light Railway suffered the same fate. The narrow-gauge platform was behind the station, not visible in this picture.

The railway land at Waterhouses has now been landscaped and the original alignment partially obliterated to make space for a car park and toilet block. The latter is visible in the centre of this 8 April 2005 picture with the railway goods shed, now converted into a tourist and information office, behind. *John K. Williams collection/HB*

WATERHOUSES: On the 2ft 6in gauge line, 2-6-4T No 2 *J. B. Earle* has just arrived at Waterhouses in about 1933 with the 3.45pm train from Hulme End.

   The area has been landscaped and the station replaced in more or less the same position by a toilet block. The former goods shed is partially visible behind it on 8 April 2005. *H. C. Casserley, John K. Williams collection/HB*

ECTON was a mile from the end of the line at Hulme End. It had once been a mining and quarrying centre but a milk factory was opened in the 1920s and provided the light railway with a major source of traffic. A siding was provided and standard-gauge milk tanks were conveyed to the factory on transporter wagons, as seen here. Unfortunately the Ecton Creamery was closed in 1932 and the local farmers sent their milk by road to a new dairy at Rowsley, so depriving the little railway of much of its revenue. This picture is looking towards Waterhouses circa 1930.

The route of the railway has long been converted into a footpath/cycleway although the section between Redhurst Halt and Butterton is used as a road for light traffic. This is the trackbed at Ecton on 8 April 2005, and surprisingly the low wooden platform edging to the right of the milk tanks is still there in a dilapidated state. *John K. Williams collection/HB*

HULME END: For ten years a short section of the Manifold Valley re-echoed to the sound of narrow-gauge steam! A local engineer, Mr Doug Blackhurst, founder of Belle Engineering Ltd at Sheen, laid portable 10¼-inch-gauge track at various fetes, traction engine rallies, etc, to raise money from fares to give to a local cancer hospice. From 1984 to 1993 10¼-inch-gauge rails were laid annually by a small dedicated band of Belle employees on part of the Leek & Manifold trackbed from Hulme End car park for about half a mile to a location called 'Apes Tor for Ecton'. The locomotive was a 10¼-inch version of 2-6-4T *J. B. Earle*, built by Mr Blackhurst in 1979, and it hauled two open and two canopied coaches also constructed by him. Trains were run at weekends during a short summer season, and the track was removed at the end of each season. This picture shows the train at Apes Tor for Ecton on 11 June 1988.

Not surprisingly as the track was portable, on 8 April 2005 there is no trace of 'Apes Tor for Ecton', and now that Mr Blackhurst is deceased, steam is, sadly, unlikely to return to this lovely valley. *John K. Williams/HB*

HULME END terminus, just over 8 miles from Waterhouses, was the most substantial station on the line and the location of the engine and carriage sheds. In this view from about 1934 there are two sidings to the left of the platform, both interlaced with standard-gauge track, and a standard-gauge open wagon can be seen on the extreme left, with the only narrow-gauge covered van prominent in front. The station building is hidden behind the coach, and to the right are the engine and carriage sheds respectively. The bunker end of No 1 *E. R. Calthrop* is visible alongside the coal stage.

The yard area has been grassed over, while the platform is now part of the approach path to the station, which has become a visitor centre. To the right of this 8 April 2005 view the engine-shed survives, now fitted with roller-shutter doors, but its current use is not known. *John K. Williams collection/HB*

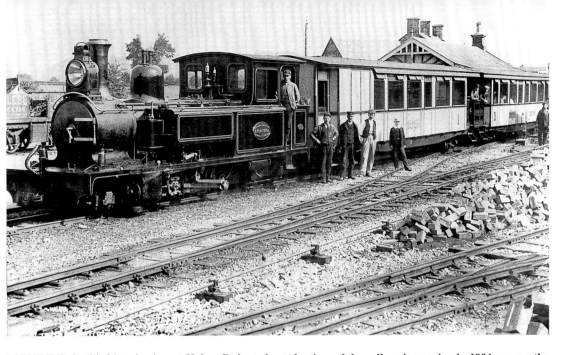

HULME END: In this historic view at Hulme End, at about the time of the railway's opening in 1904, we see the brand-new Kitson-built *E. R. Calthrop* and two of the bogie coaches, a Brake Composite and a 3rd Class vehicle behind. Four coaches were built by the Electric Railway & Tramway Carriage Works at Preston in 1904, like the locomotives to the design of Mr Calthrop. Note that the two locomotives each had a combined name, number and maker's plate and were appropriately named after Everard Calthrop, Chief Mechanical Engineer, and John Earle, the Resident Engineer. One of these attractive combined plates, *J. B. Earle*, was sold a few years ago at Sheffield Railwayana Auctions for £20,000. *John K. Williams collection*

GRINDON: This circa 1920 photograph shows a unique feature of the Leek & Manifold, in that it was the only railway in Great Britain to use transporter wagons. This mixed train is leaving Grindon towards Hulme End with two transporters conveying standard-gauge wagons. Four transporter wagons were built in two batches of two by Cravens Railway Carriage & Wagon Co in 1904 and 1907/8, followed by one more from Stoke LMS Works in 1923. *John K. Williams collection*

Churnet Valley line

RUSHTON: The NSR opened the Churnet Valley line from North Rode, in Cheshire on the main line to Macclesfield, to Uttoxeter, a distance of 27¾ miles, on 13 July 1849. Coming south, the first station in Staffordshire was Rushton. This picture shows the station, built in the attractive NSR Jacobean style, with Fowler Class 4P 2-6-4T No 42319 arriving with a Macclesfield to Uttoxeter train circa 1954.

The station has now become an attractive residence; on 26 March 2005 the platforms remain and the trackbed forms part of the garden. *W. A. Camwell, Martin Welch collection/HB*

RUDYARD LAKE/CLIFFE PARK HALT was situated at the north end of Rudyard Lake and opened on 1 May 1905 after the NSR had purchased the Cliffe Park Estate and turned it into a golf course; it was called Rudyard Lake until renamed by the LMS in 1926. No 42363, one of the big Fowler-designed 2-6-4Ts that were regular performers on this line, is seen pulling away from the Halt with the 3.44pm Macclesfield to Uttoxeter train on 30 September 1959.

There is no trace of the station on 26 March 2005. Out of the picture to the left, railings remain leading down from the overbridge in the background and, surprisingly, the dark bush on the right is still the same shape, having hardly grown at all! *Michael Mensing/HB*

RUDYARD station, once called Rudyard Lake, is seen here looking towards Leek in about 1930. This station was at the south end of Rudyard Lake, an artificial lake constructed to feed water into the canal systems and completed about 1799. Nearby was the house occupied by the Lake Superintendent, which the NSR bought in 1850 and converted into a hotel. The railway actively promoted the lake and surrounding area as pleasure grounds, with considerable success.

The only remaining evidence of the standard-gauge station today is the stone wall on the right, which was adjacent to the platform signal box in the 'past' picture. As can be seen, there is still a railway station here, now with a car park, the home of the 10¼-inch-gauge Rudyard Lake Steam Railway. The station is on the left and 2-4-2T *Excalibur* (built by Exmoor in 1993) is waiting to depart northwards with a train to Hunthouse Wood, a distance of nearly 1½ miles, on 26 March 2005. *John K. Williams collection/HB*

On 26 March 2005 the 13.40 train to Hunthouse Wood, behind 2-4-2T *Excalibur*, stands in the station. The waiting shelter on the left is placed on the up platform of the NSR station and the narrow-gauge lines are laid on the old trackbed. *HB*

LEEK was the principal intermediate station and the only town on the Churnet Valley line, and the station layout is seen in this excellent 1963 view looking north. On the left is the coal yard with the gasworks and gas-holder in the left background; the station is in the centre behind Fowler Class 4F 0-6-0 No 44079, which is shunting, and the goods yard is behind the signal box on the right. The passenger service north of Leek ceased in November 1960, and workmen's trains south to Uttoxeter on 4 January 1965. Goods trains ran until 15 June 1964.

It is now impossible to comprehend that a thriving and busy railway was once located here. Only the three white houses on the skyline and the tall poplars to their right identify the location, and the minor road overbridge from which both pictures were taken is still in use. The railway site is now the Barnfields Industrial Estate, with the rear of Safeway (now Morrisons) supermarket prominent on the right of this 23 March 2005 view. *Phil Waterfield/HB*

LEEK BROOK JUNCTION is seen looking south, with a sand train having emerged from Cheddleton Tunnel. In earlier times this was known as Leek Brook South Junction until the North Junction, which provided a direct line from Leek to Waterhouses, was closed in 1964. The train, 8K02 from Oakamoor to Worksop and St Helens on 10 April 1984, is hauled by Class 25 Nos 25176 and 25210 and will reverse here before proceeding to Stoke on the line going to the right (see also page 84).

The dormant tracks remain, with the signal box partly hidden by trees. Network Rail has fenced off the railway on the other side, which is now at the northern end of the flourishing Churnet Valley Railway. CVR trains travel up to this location in order for the locomotives to run round their trains, and the rear of a CVR train, hauled by Class 33 No 33102, can just be seen heading towards Cheddleton Tunnel on 26 March 2005. *Paul D. Shannon/HB*

The interior of Leek Brook Junction signal box, with signalman Mr Ken Faulkner on duty, was also photographed 10 April 1984. The diagram above the McKenzie & Holland lever frame shows the simplified layout effected by BR when the remnant of the Churnet Valley line, to serve the sand siding at Oakamoor, was reduced to siding status and singled in October 1968. *Paul D. Shannon*

CHEDDLETON was another station built in the NSR Jacobean style. The first view is looking north towards Cheddleton Tunnel on 4 April 1958.

This second picture was taken on 27 August 1986 in the line's later BR days, showing the attractive location despite the removal of the down line in the early days of the CVR before the preservation society was able to acquire the track. Coming south are Class 20 Nos 20121 and 20188 with an empty sand train, number 6K56, the 10.05 Ravenhead to Oakamoor.

Today Cheddleton station is the headquarters of the Churnet Valley Railway and the station is thankfully secured for posterity. At the present time the only running line is through the up platform, and while the down platform is accessible to passengers for refreshments, the track is only a siding. Somewhat incongruously, the down home signal is placed in the trackbed, but the engineer's bogie coach, blocking the view, has been removed since this photograph was taken on 26 March 2005. *John K. Williams/Paul D. Shannon/HB*

CONSALL: In the deepest part of the Churnet Valley a small station was opened at Consall Forge on 3 March 1902, adjacent to the Caldon Canal. This is the view looking north towards Leek in about 1910, but what is not visible is the canal immediately on the other side of the railings on the right, so close in fact that the waiting shelter is cantilevered out over the it.

The station has been beautifully restored by the CVR and on 26 March 2005 the up platform with its new waiting shelter, again cantilevered out over the canal, was nearing completion ready for the new season. The up line is also in position so that the station can provide a passing loop for CVR trains. *John K. Williams collection/HB*

KINGSLEY & FROGHALL station is seen in about 1910 looking north towards the bridge carrying the main Stoke to Ashbourne road over the railway. The tranquillity of the Churnet Valley was disrupted in this area by heavy industry, and the smoke from one of the chimneys of Thomas Bolton & Sons' copper and brass works can be seen in the background.

When the CVR purchased the track from Leek Brook Junction to south of Kingsley & Froghall from BR, only the derelict platforms remained at the latter station. In 2002 the preservation company started to build a completely new station on the up platform in the traditional style of the NSR and it was officially opened by Pete Waterman on 20 September 2003. Seen here on 3 April 2005, in addition to the usual railway facilities, a particularly attractive tea-room has been opened, and its reputation and ambiance is spreading well beyond the railway. *John K. Williams collection/HB*

OAKAMOOR: This delightful scene emphasises the beauty of the Churnet Valley and the attractive stations built by the NSR for the railway. Fairburn Class 4P 2-6-4T No 42081 is starting away with an afternoon train from Macclesfield to Uttoxeter in 1962.

On 28 March 2005 only the platforms remain and the station area is now a car park for people to use the 'Old Churnet Railway' walk to Alton, 1½ miles to the south. *Phil Waterfield/HB*

OAKAMOOR: Immediately to the north of the platform there was a siding, branching to the right, to the Thomas Bolton & Sons copper wire works. This business once provided the railway with useful traffic, and in 1917 the NSR provided a small battery-electric locomotive to shunt this siding. Following its withdrawal it has been preserved, first at Shugborough Hall and now at the National Railway Museum, York. Here, at the other extreme of motive power, Stanier Class 8F 2-8-0 No 48106 is shunting wagons on to the branch in 1962, a year before the Oakamoor works were closed.

In the present-day picture, taken on 28 March 2005, all the track has since been removed but the route of the siding provides one of several footpaths around Oakamoor. *Phil Waterfield/ HB*

The ornate level-crossing keeper's house, also photographed on 28 March 2005, has become a most attractive residence, while to the left, in the trees, is the southern portal of the 550-yard-long Oakamoor Tunnel, now fenced off. *HB*

ALTON TOWERS station was another architectural delight, influenced by the fact that nearby was the residence of the Earl of Shrewsbury. Originally just Alton, it was renamed Alton Towers in 1954 to reflect that Alton Towers gardens had become a popular destination for visitors, and regular excursion trains were operated to it. This picture shows an everyday service train, the 11.25am from Leek to Uttoxeter, hauled by Fowler Class 4P 2-6-4T No 42323 on 19 August 1961. The down platform, on the left, is now completely covered by trees so this comparison view, taken on 28 March 2005, is slightly to the right of the 'past' picture, but the main buildings and the up platform remain, as do the entrance steps on the right. *Michael Mensing/HB*

ALTON TOWERS: Looking south from the down platform, a train can be seen standing in the bay platform on the extreme right. Another Fowler 2-6-4T, No 42381, is arriving with a train from Uttoxeter to Leek on 2 July 1960.

The down platform and bay lie hidden in trees and undergrowth, but the up side is in good condition and the station is partly use as a hostel for hikers, although closed at the time of this visit on 28 March 2005. *Martin Welch collection/HB*

DENSTONE station building had originally been built as a crossing keeper's house for the opening of the railway in 1849, but when Denstone College was opened in 1873 a station was required, so the keeper's house was altered to provide station facilities. This view is looking south towards Uttoxeter in about 1955.

On 28 March 2005 the platforms remain but the buildings have gone. The station master's house, just visible in the 'past' picture behind the signal and across the road, is still a residence. The level-crossing gates have been replaced with field gates and a rather ugly house has been built across the trackbed on the far side of the road. *V. & R. Anderson collection/HB*

ROCESTER: Near Rocester the River Churnet meets the River Dove flowing from the north, and likewise Rocester was also a junction for the NSR branch to Ashbourne, opened in May 1852, which subsequently connected with the LNWR line from Buxton. This photograph, looking north, shows Stanier Class 4P 2-6-4T No 42567 entering the station with a train to Uttoxeter on 17 June 1958.

The railway in this area has been completely obliterated by massive development of the factory and ancillary activities of J. C. Bamford, the renowned manufacturer of earth-moving plant and machinery. In addition, Bamford's has gone to much effort to landscape the ground nearby, with corresponding alterations to the road layout. With the help of local historian and former Bamford's employee, Mr Roy Burnett, on 3 April 2005 it was established that the car park of Bamford's sports & social club is in the location of the former railway scene. *Hugh Davies, John K. Williams collection/HB*

Stoke to Uttoxeter and the Cheadle Railway

FENTON, another of the 'Six Towns', was the first station on the line from Stoke to Uttoxeter. The first station opened with the railway in 1848, but was replaced by this one in 1906. This 1948 view, looking east towards Uttoxeter, shows the substantial awnings and wide down platform. The station was closed on 6 February 1961.

On 23 March 2005 the equivalent picture had to be taken from the road bridge to the west of the station. The only remaining evidence is part of the brick wall, in the centre of the picture, which can also be seen at the end of the platform in the 'past' photograph. *John K. Williams collection/HB*

NORMACOT is seen here in an old postcard view of about 1890, looking east. This station was not opened until 1 November 1882 when the Potteries suburbs were expanding east of Longton. The station was a rather plain wooden-framed building, one of only two on the NSR (the other being at Horninglow, Burton-on-Trent). The Stoke-bound train is being hauled by Class 'B' 2-4-0T No 23, built at Stoke in 1886 and withdrawn in 1928.

There is no trace of the station, which was closed on 2 March 1964, the buildings of which would have been near the up Longton distant signal, seen in the background on 23 March 2005. *John K. Williams collection/HB*

NORMACOT: On 29 October 1966 the Railway Correspondence & Travel Society ran the 'Stoke Area Brake-van Tour' with Ivatt Class 2 2-6-2T No 41204, well turned out by Stockport Edgeley shed, hauling ten 20-ton brake-vans from Stoke to Cheadle and later up to the Caldon Quarry branch. Here No 41204 is passing the closed Normacot station on the 1 in 102 climb to Meir Tunnel en route to Cheadle.

It was not possible to photograph at platform level on 23 March 2005 as it is no longer there, or accessible, so the view is from a footbridge at the east end of the station, from which can be seen the houses in the background of both pictures. *Martin Welch/HB*

MEIR station was situated in a deep cutting to the east of Meir Tunnel (847 yards), and this picture is looking towards Stoke in about 1910. The station was closed on 7 November 1966.

The tunnel is just visible through the encroaching trees on 23 March 2005, but there is no evidence that there was once a station in the cutting below. *V. & R. Anderson collection/HB*

BLYTHE BRIDGE was the location of an impressive signal box, which controlled the level-crossing over the main Stoke to Derby road, but by the time of this photograph the station building has been partially let to a hairdresser, but at least the attractive building still stands as an identifiable piece of NSR railway architecture. This picture is looking east on 29 March 1980, with the former goods shed in the centre of the photograph.

The signal box and station buildings, in the name of BR progress, have been demolished, although the station, in its basic form, is still open, as seen on 20 March 2005. The former goods shed remains as part of a builders merchant's yard, and the level-crossing is now protected by automatic lifting barriers. *John K. Williams collection*

CRESSWELL was one of the original stations, opening with the line in 1848, but it became the junction when the Cheadle Railway opened its short line in 1892. This is the view in about 1959 looking west towards Stoke, showing the substantial station and signal box protecting the level-crossing over a minor road. The station was closed to passengers on 7 November 1966.

There is no trace of the station on 23 March 2005 and the crossing is now protected by automatic barriers. Altogether a depressing scene, at least there is still a railway service between Stoke and Uttoxeter. *V. R. Anderson*

TEAN: The Cheadle Railway branch left the main line just east of Cresswell station and there was only one intermediate station, seen here in about 1910. Originally called Totmonslow and opened for traffic on 7 November 1892, it was renamed Tean in December 1906 after the large village of Upper Tean, a mile to the east, following which part of the station building from Keele Park, on the Market Drayton branch, was erected on the platform. This picture, looking towards Cheadle, shows the neat station and, beyond, the road overbridge carrying the Stoke to Derby main road, which passed through the village. This little station was closed to all traffic on 1 June 1953.

The Cheadle Railway was purchased by the NSR on 1 January 1907 and the branch remained open after the closure of Tean station until, finally, regular goods traffic ceased in 1986, so it is surprising to see that the track and platform are still in situ today, although nature is rapidly gaining control. 28 March 2005. *John K. Williams collection/HB*

TEAN: The passenger train service to Cheadle continued until 17 June 1963, and here a Class 104 DMU passes the closed Tean station working the 1.35pm Cheadle to Stoke service on 19 August 1961. By now the old platform is being used as a very unsightly scrapyard.

As seen on the previous page, the track and platform remain on 28 March 2005, but at least all the scrap and rubbish has been removed, so enabling nature to quietly continue to take over. *Michael Mensing/HB*

CHEADLE: The railway eventually reached Cheadle on 1 January 1901, but a diversion line to avoid the 977-yard-long tunnel under a ridge of high ground to the south-west of the town, which needed much maintenance, was opened on 26 November 1933. This picture shows the single-platform station at Cheadle looking towards the buffer stops on 7 May 1960.

On 28 March 2005, although much of the branch track remains, disused, the rails at the Cheadle end have gone and the land sold for redevelopment. The station tracks have now become 'The Sidings', a cul-de-sac of houses. *John K. Williams collection/HB*

CHEADLE: On a dull day in 1962 Fowler Class 4F No 44499 is running round its stock at Cheadle before taking its three-coach passenger train back to Stoke.

The location was identified on 28 March 2005 using the house just visible above No 44499's chimney, which can also just be glimpsed above the digger on the left. The new houses at the end of 'The Sidings' straddle the old trackbed. *Phil Waterfield/HB*

LEIGH: Back on the Uttoxeter line, the next station east of Cresswell was at Leigh, seen here on 19 August 1961 with a very dirty Class 5XP 4-6-0 No 45631 *Tanganyika* passing the station with an excursion train thought to be from North Wales heading towards Derby.

Leigh station was closed to passengers on 7 November 1966, two years after goods facilities had been withdrawn. Other than a very small piece of platform edging by the level-crossing on the left-hand side, on 28 March 2005 there was no trace of the station. The station land, now behind the tall trees, is owned by Steve Foster's crane hire business. *Michael Mensing*

Steve Foster bought Leigh signal box, minus its frame, after closure and has now positioned it in his yard. The Stoke to Derby line is immediately behind the trees in this 28 March 2005 view. *HB*

UTTOXETER: A Class 120 three-car DMU leaves Uttoxeter as the 1.35pm Lincoln (St Marks) to Crewe service on 21 April 1979. The unit is passing the site of the West Junction with the now unstaffed station behind it. This was the second station built in the market town, opened in 1881, the original 1848 station being a quarter of a mile east at the junction with the Churnet Valley line. This station provided platforms for the Churnet Valley trains giving direct access from the west curve, and the curving station roof can be seen above the middle coach of the DMU. The Churnet Valley workmen's trains finally ceased on 4 January 1965 and, as seen here, the trackbed and platforms have been sold for commercial use.

Exactly the same position could not be repeated on 28 March 2005 as the present road bridge is a little further away from the now stark minimal platforms. However, there is a reasonably frequent weekday Stoke to Derby DMU service calling at the station, which is particularly well situated for Uttoxeter racecourse. *Michael Mensing/HB*

Stafford to Uttoxeter

STAFFORD COMMON: The least significant, in mileage terms, of the three pre-Grouping companies operating in North Staffordshire was the Great Northern Railway, having an outpost many miles west of its traditional territory. Originally built as the Stafford & Uttoxeter Railway in 1867 and absorbed by the GNR in 1881, it reached Stafford by means of running powers over the NSR from Egginton Junction (3 miles north of Burton-on-Trent) as far as Bromshall Junction (2 miles west of Uttoxeter), thence over its own track to Stafford, where it rented a bay platform from the LNWR. This is a well-known picture of Stafford Common station showing an ex-GNR 4-4-0, LNER Class 'D20' No 4399, waiting to depart with a train to Derby Friargate or Nottingham via Uttoxeter in about 1925.

The platform edges remain on 29 March 2005, but the trackbed has become a footpath/cycleway between Doxey Road and Beaconside. *John K. Williams collection/HB*

STAFFORD COMMON: Looking east under the station overbridge, we see the sparse platforms after the passenger service had been withdrawn in 1939, although the line remained open for goods traffic until 1951, the date of this photograph. From the main-line junction at Stafford to RAF 16 Maintenance Unit on the edge of the town, a distance of 2 miles, military traffic continued to be conveyed until 1 December 1975.

The station buildings astride the running lines have gone, and this picture was taken on 29 March 2005 from beneath Common Road overbridge, which had been adjacent to the station, again showing the platforms at this end. *R. M. Casserley collection/HB*

INGESTRE FOR WESTON: The Stafford to Uttoxeter railway was closed as a through line on 5 March 1951, and six years later, on 23 March 1957, the Stephenson Locomotive Society organised a final run before abandonment. The rear of the three-coach train, hauled by Ivatt Class 2 2-6-2T No 41224, is seen during a stop at Ingestre for Weston station.

The area has been redeveloped and road access to the former railway realigned. With the help of a local resident the neat grass adjacent to the Village Hall was identified as where the station was situated, looking in the direction of Uttoxeter on 9 April 2005. *R. M. Casserley/HB*

CHARTLEY: The SLS special of 23 March 1957 has moved 2 miles to the next station, where again the passengers have alighted to inspect the location. Having not seen passengers for 18 years, the buildings seem in remarkably good – and not vandalised – condition.

Endeavouring to look over the railway bridge from which the 'past' picture was taken, on 9 April 2005 the photographer was confronted by an impenetrable mass of bushes. However, on exploring at track level from the road by the Village Hall, and forcing your way through more vegetation, most of both platform edges can be seen.
R. M. Casserley/HB

GRINDLEY was the last station from Stafford before GNR trains passed on to NSR metals at Bromshall Junction. This photograph from about 1905 shows the neat layout, seen from the Stafford end.

The road overbridge has been filled in, and where the 1905 picture was taken is now a large horse manure muck-heap. This picture was taken from the bridge and shows the cutting and station area full of rubble and soil on 9 April 2005. *John K. Williams collection/HB*

UTTOXETER station had four platforms, and on 10 April 1930 Class 3F 0-6-0 No 3225 passes through the station with a mixed goods train on the Derby line. To the right, the lady and boy seem to be carrying very large baskets and behind them the platforms for the Churnet Valley and Ashbourne trains are visible.

Two years later, an LNER train from Stafford to Derby Friargate is seen on arrival at Uttoxeter hauled by a former GNR 0-6-0, LNER Class 'J3' No 4032, on 2 April 1932. This engine was built by Dubs & Co in 1896 and withdrawn in 1936.

The third picture shows Class 170 two-car DMU No 170508 arriving as the 10.08 Crewe to Skegness service on 5 April 2005. The contrast between the station facilities offered today and in the 1930s is startling. *John K. Williams collection (2)/HB*

INDEX OF LOCATIONS

Alton Towers 104-106

Badnall Wharf 14
Barlaston & Tittensor 53
Black Bull 77
Blythe Bridge 113
Bradnop 85
Burslem 66

Caldon Low 86-87
Chartley 124
Cheadle 117-118
Cheddleton 99
Cliff Park Halt *see* Rudyard
    Lake
Cobridge 67
Cold Meece branch 56-58
Colwich 30-34
Consall 100
Cresswell 114

Denstone 107

Ecton 90
Endon 81
Etruria 44
Etruria Junction 70-71

Fenton 109
Fenton Manor 80
Ford Green 78

Grange Junction, Etruria 44
Great Bridgeford 17

Grindley 125
Grindon 93

Hanley 68-69
Harecastle *see* Kidsgrove
    Central
Harecastle Tunnel 39-42
Hulme End 91-93

Ingestre for Weston 123

Kidsgrove Central 38
Kidsgrove Liverpool Road
    61
Kidsgrove Market St Halt 62
Kingsley & Froghall 101

Leek 97
Leek Brook Junction 83-84,
    98
Leigh 119
Liverpool Road Halt 74
Longport 43

Madeley 9
Meir 112
Milford & Brockton 28
Milton Junction 79

Newcastle Junction, Stoke
    72
Newcastle-under-Lyme 73
Newchapel & Goldenhill 63
Newfields branch 64

Normacot 110-111
Norton Bridge 15-16

Oakamoor 102-103

Rocester 108
Rudyard 96
Rudyard Lake 95
Rugeley Trent Valley 35-37
Rushton 94

Sandon 59
Shugborough Tunnel 29
Silverdale 75-76
Stafford 18-27
    shed 20-21
Stafford Common 121-122
Standon Bridge 12-13
Stoke-on-Trent 6, 45-50, 72
    shed 50
Stone 4-5, 54-55

Tean 115-116
Trentham 51
Trentham Park 52
Tunstall 65

Uttoxeter 120, 126-127

Wall Grange & Longsdon 82
Waterhouses 88-89
Weston & Ingestre 60
Whitmore water troughs 10-
    11